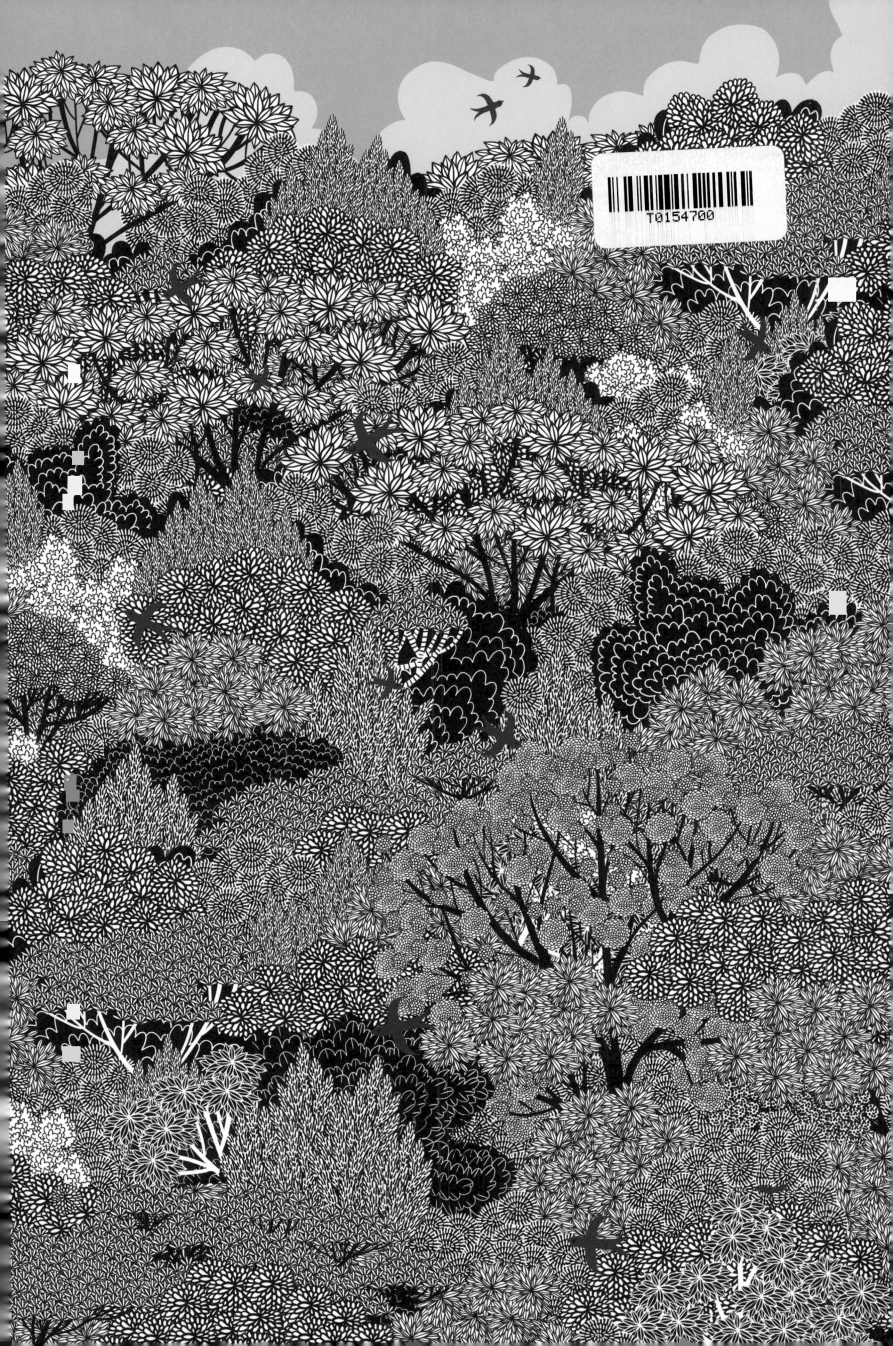

Did you know that trees talk? They do! They speak to each other and will talk to you too, if you listen.

First published in France under the title *Un arbre, une histoire*, © Actes Sud, Paris, 2018.
Written by Cécile Benoist
Illustrated by Charlotte Gastaut
Translated into English by Sylvia Rucker
English language edition edited by Julie Merberg
Published in English by Downtown Bookworks Inc.
© 2019 Downtown Bookworks
All rights reserved.
Printed in China, September 2019
ISBN: 978-1-941367-99-5
10 9 8 7 6 5 4 3 2 1

downtown bookworks

Downtown Bookworks Inc.
265 Canal Street, New York, NY 10013
www.downtownbookworks.com

EVERY TREE
has a story

Cécile Benoist   Charlotte Gastaut

CONTENTS

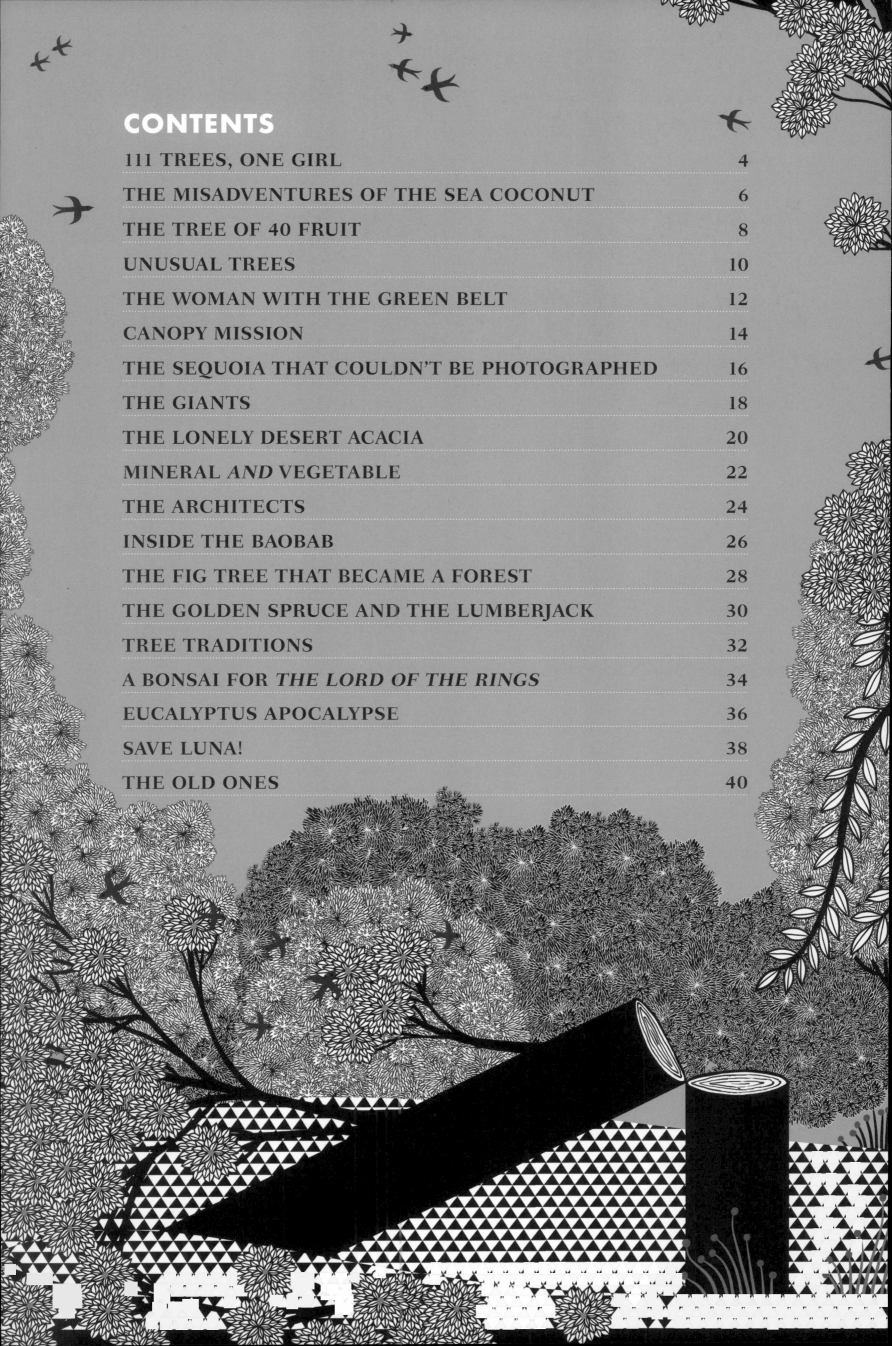

111 TREES, ONE GIRL

Every time a baby girl is born in Piplantri, India, the village celebrates by planting 111 trees. It wasn't always this way, though. For hundreds of years, poor families in India would hope for baby boys. A girl was considered a burden to the family because her parents would someday have to pay a *dowry* (money and gifts) to her husband's family. That was the way things worked.

But in 2006, the daughter of the village chief died. Shyam was heartbroken because he loved and missed his daughter Kiran so much. To honor her, he planted a burflower tree, a symbol of love. He would visit the tree often, and sitting under its shade, he thought a lot about Kiran. And he got to thinking about how all girls should be cherished.

Shyam decided that every time a girl was born, not only would the villagers come together to plant trees, but they would also contribute money to be saved for when that baby girl grew up. He made a rule that girls could not marry before the age of 18 so they could focus on their education instead.

At first, the villagers followed the new rules because their chief told them to. But they quickly realized that the birth of a little girl was cause for celebration! They happily planted rosewood, mango, and Indian gooseberry trees, and soon the dry, brown hills surrounding the village became lush and green.

The only problem was that all of these new fruit trees attracted termites. The villagers didn't give up. Luckily, they had discovered that termites stay away from aloe plants. So they planted a ring of aloe plants around each tree to keep the pests away. In 10 years' time, hundreds of thousands of aloe plants were thriving, protecting tens of thousands of trees. Aloe plants produce healing juice and gel. The women of Piplantri began to harvest and sell the aloe gel, providing them with a source of income.

Although the first tree was planted out of grief, in nurturing the trees and the girls of Piplantri, the people transformed their landscape as well as their way of life.

THE MISADVENTURES OF THE SEA COCONUT

When European explorers began to sail around the world, they would see enormous sea coconuts floating in the Indian Ocean. Not only were the coconuts gigantic, but they also came in pairs. Sailors could not imagine where these strange double nuts came from! Maybe there was a mythical underwater tree?

In the 17th century, the explorers finally discovered the source of these unusual coconuts. They came from the *Lodoicea maldivica* tree, which grows only on two tiny islands: Praslin Island and Curieuse Island, part of a cluster of islands called the Seychelles. These beautiful green islands are surrounded by turquoise sea, about 1,000 miles off the coast of Africa.

The islanders would gather the coconuts after they fell to the ground. They believed that the fruit found inside of these huge double nuts had healing properties. Plus, they could sell the coconuts: The nuts were so large and funny-looking that tourists visiting the islands were willing to pay crazy prices for them.

Soon all of the nuts that had fallen to the ground were gone, and the islanders began to climb the trees to pick them. Since each nut takes six to seven years to grow to full size, they were picked much faster than they could grow. Without their coconuts, the trees grew weak and died. Without the trees, these islands would lose their unique treasure. Eventually, the government had to step in to protect the trees.

Now instead of picking and poaching, islanders have learned to protect their natural resources.

THE TREE OF 40 FRUIT

Sam Van Aken was raised on a farm in Pennsylvania, so it was not surprising that when he grew up to be an artist, he dreamed about creating a spectacular tree. This tree would have blossoms of many colors, and it would bear different types of fruit. He wanted this special tree to grow stone fruit—peaches, plums, nectarines, apricots, and cherries. He wasn't thinking of painting a picture of this tree. He wanted to create an *actual* tree!

One day while searching for the perfect tree and fruit, Sam discovered an old orchard that was home to hundreds of rare, ancient stone fruit trees. The owners were going to tear out the orchard. He bought it.

And then he went to work. First, he created a calendar so he could keep track of the exact flowering dates of close to 250 varieties of stone fruit. Then he put his farming skills to work and began to *graft* different trees onto one *stock* tree. (Grafting means taking a bud from one tree and connecting it to the trunk or branch of a related tree called the stock tree.) He was careful to choose a range of fruits and different colored blossoms, and also to ensure that the tree would bloom from May to October. Over the course of five years, he grafted dozens of new branches onto his original tree. His masterpiece was finally taking shape!

At first, it looked like an ordinary green tree. But in the spring, five years after he began his work, it was bursting with gorgeous, fragrant pink, white, red, and purple blossoms. And from late summer to fall, the branches were heavy with peaches, plums, nectarines, apricots, and cherries—all on the same tree. He'd created his very own living work of art.

A thing of incredible beauty, the tree is also a form of conservation—Sam is preserving ancient and native varieties of fruit that are really difficult to find elsewhere. His first Tree of 40 Fruit was so stunning and successful that he continues to grow *hybrid* (combination) fruit trees all around the United States, spreading the idea of celebrating diversity.

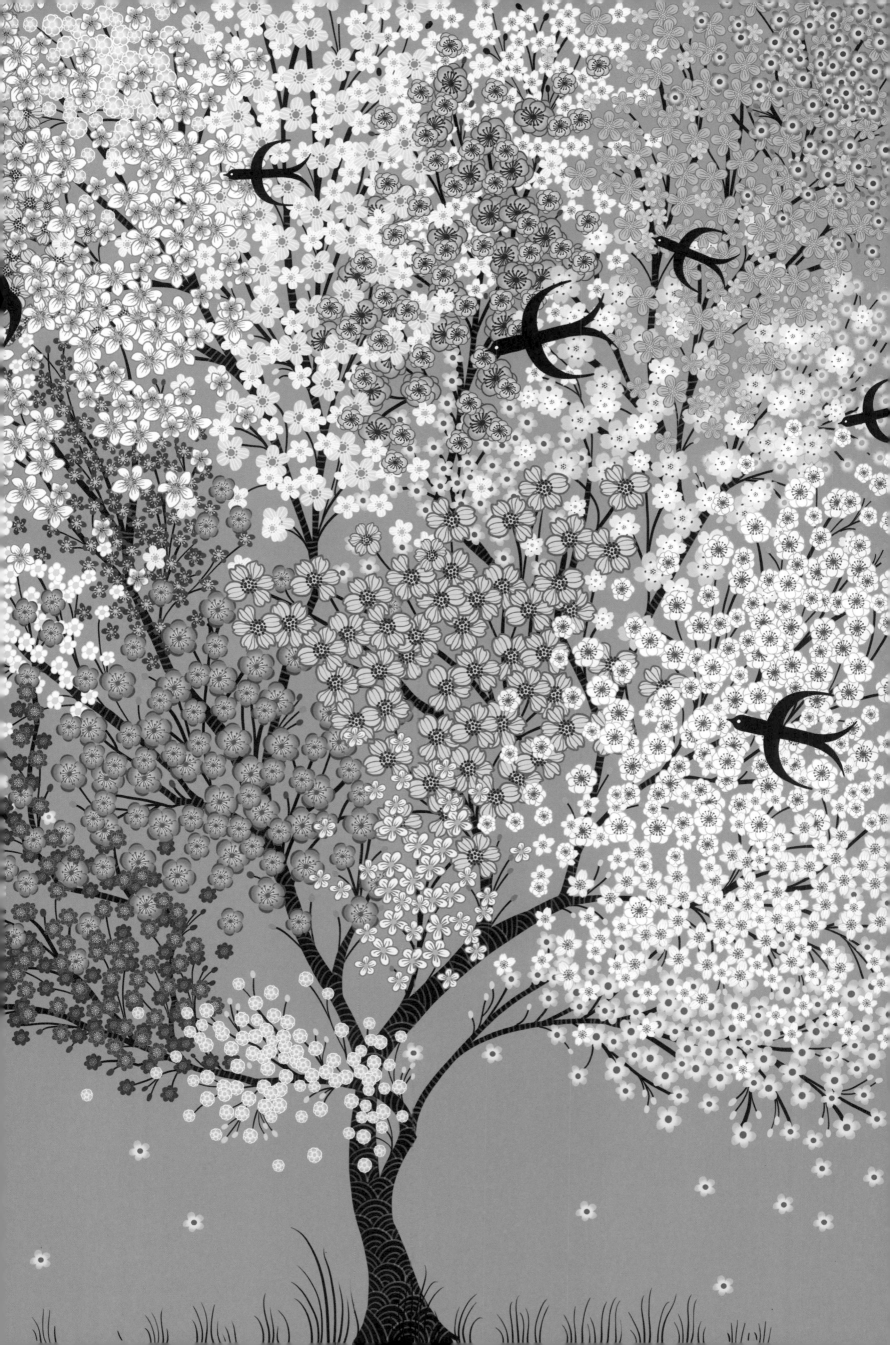

UNUSUAL TREES

THE ARTIST
The bark of the rainbow eucalyptus peels at different times of the year, exposing its dark green core. As the tree matures, this core turns blue, then purple, orange, brown . . . Each rainbow eucalyptus has its own unique palette and keeps changing color over its entire life.

THE MOVER
The walking palm doesn't really walk, but it does move—as much as 3 feet a year. How exactly does a tree move? It leans to find light in the dark tropical forest or to right itself after another tree has fallen over onto it. Sometimes it leans too much and falls over. When that happens, it grows an extra "stilt root" in the place where it fell. The older parts of the trunk die, while the part with the new supporting roots grows in the place where it fell.

THE BLEEDING TREE
The dragon's blood tree's strange umbrella shape is not the weirdest thing about it. Its bright red sap is. In ancient days, this bloodred sap was used to dye wool. It was also used as medicine to stop bleeding and promote healing.

THE BOTTLE TREE
The palo borracho tree, which grows in Latin America, has an unusual trunk shaped like a bottle. It is covered with prickly cones, and its fruit look like large eggs.

THE TREE THAT'S NEVER THIRSTY
Nobody knows how the Tree of Life, planted more than 400 years ago, has been able to survive in the Arabian Desert on the island of Bahrain. Yet year after year, its leaves are green. A type of mesquite, it may have super-powered roots which can somehow draw water from deep, deep down or even from the sand. Or maybe, as some locals believe, it is protected by the mythical water god.

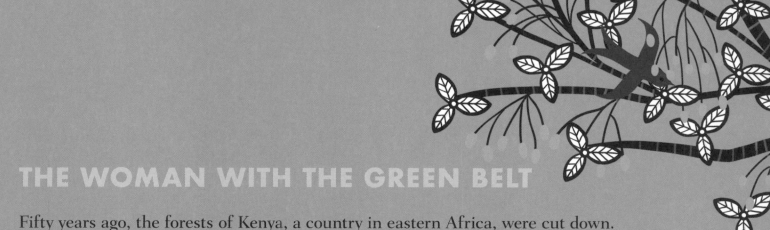

THE WOMAN WITH THE GREEN BELT

Fifty years ago, the forests of Kenya, a country in eastern Africa, were cut down. The wood was sold, turned into paper and buildings, or burned as firewood. The leaders of the country became rich, so they were happy. But the people who lived off the land were struggling. It was hard to grow anything in the soil. There was very little water. And there was no firewood when the weather turned cold.

Then Wangari Maathai, a brilliant young scholar, had a dream. She remembered the lush green valleys of her childhood, before the forests were cut down. She knew that *reforesting the land* (planting new trees) was important both for the land and for the people who lived there. She decided to get other women to help her realize her dream by planting trees. And she would make sure that the women were paid for their work—helping them too. With jobs and money, the women could become independent.

On June 5, 1977, hundreds of women paraded through the capital, Nairobi. They headed for a large park where they planted seven trees in honor of seven famous Kenyans. Important business and government leaders looked on. The first "green belt" was planted.

Wangari then traveled throughout the country to convince more people that it was important to plant trees. Her message: "When we plant trees, we plant the seeds of peace and hope."

In the more than 40 years since she began sowing seeds, more than 52 million seedlings have been planted, thanks to Wangari and what is now known as the Green Belt Movement. Her dream transformed both the land and the people of Kenya.

CANOPY MISSION

Francis Hallé is a *botanist* (a scientist who studies plants and trees). In 1974, he was in South America exploring the Guyanese forest with a group of students. Hundred-foot-tall (and taller!) trees towered over them.

"I bet there's a lot going on up there!"

"Wouldn't it be amazing to see what's happening on the treetops?"

"If only we could fly over them," they said.

The students may have been joking around, but the young botanist couldn't stop thinking about studying the *canopy* (the tops) of the oldest trees. He visited a hot-air balloon factory in France where he found out that it would indeed be possible for him to float over the treetops in a hot-air balloon. But he would need a pilot to accompany him.

Francis attended a gathering of balloon pilots where he met Dany Cleyet-Marrel. He spoke with Dany about flying a balloon over faraway forests. Though the two adventurers went their separate ways, Dany did not stop thinking about his new botanist friend.

A few years later, Dany came up with an idea that he thought just might work. If he could replace a hot-air balloon's hard basket with something inflatable, like a raft, he could make a soft "tree landing."

While Dany was thinking about landing on the treetops, an architect named Gilles Ebersolt was developing a large net on a soft frame that could be unfurled on treetops. This net would make the perfect landing surface.

So the botanist, the pilot, and the architect put their heads and their inventions together and tested a balloon landing on a tree canopy. At last, Francis was able to explore life at the tippy top of the forest, just the way he had imagined.

THE SEQUOIA THAT COULDN'T BE PHOTOGRAPHED

Sequoia National Park in California is a paradise of giant sequoia trees. One of the largest specimens in the world, the President Tree, is found there. This tree is so tall that it's impossible to look at the whole plant at once. And for a long time, it was also impossible to consider taking a photo of the entire tree. How could anyone possibly take a picture of an enormous tree in the heart of an extremely dense forest packed with other giants?

But there are always artists who like to rise to challenges and seize opportunities.

In 2012, a team of scientists was doing research in the park. Naturally, the President Tree captured all of their attention. With sophisticated tools, they were able to measure its height down to the inch. Their results were dizzying: The tree was 247 feet tall. And it had 82,000 pine cones and two billion leaves.

Michael Nichols, the winner of many photography awards, had already photographed giant trees for *National Geographic* magazine. He did not want to miss out on this rare opportunity! And he knew just how to tackle this challenge.

He arrived on the scene after the scientists had completed their survey. His team attached cords to the President Tree and to the nearby trees. Michael had a very precise image in mind. Everyone was waiting for the sky to clear, the snow to melt, and the fog to lift . . . but when the snow started to fall again, it was time to shoot some pictures.

A total of 126 of Michael's pictures were assembled to create the final image of the President Tree. This image was later printed on a five-page foldout spread in *National Geographic*.

Before leaving the forest, Michael put on a helmet and a harness, attached himself to a cord, and climbed up into the high branches of the President Tree for one last look—without his camera, "just to say goodbye."

THE GIANTS

THE LARGEST
The largest tree in the world, known as the General Sherman Tree, is located in Sequoia National Park in California. At 275 feet tall, its trunk has a volume of 52,500 cubic feet. And it's still growing after 2,000 years!

THE TALLEST
Hyperion has grown up in Redwood National Park in California, where there are many giant sequoias (specifically, giant coastal redwoods). Its *crown* (the top part of a tree) reaches close to 380 feet high, which makes it the tallest tree in the world.

THE BROADEST CROWN
Major Oak's branches are more than 92 feet long and spread out like tentacles, held up by thinner stems. With its strange, twisted shape and impressive age of 800 years, this tree is beloved in England. It holds court in the heart of Sherwood Forest, and some people claim that its trunk was once a hiding place for Robin Hood.

THE WIDEST
In the Mexican village of Santa María del Tule, life revolves around a very fat Montezuma cypress. The 134-foot-tall Tule Tree boasts a trunk that is an astonishing 138 feet around. Children like to look for animal outlines on the gnarled bark of this tree, the stoutest in the world.

THE MOST DAZZLING
Every fall, near the Gu Guanyin Buddhist Temple in the Zhongnan Mountains of China, a maidenhair tree leaves a fascinating gold carpet at its base. Roughly 1,400 years old, this tree is a *Ginkgo biloba*, a species that has thrived since the time of the dinosaurs.

THE LONELY DESERT ACACIA

The Ténéré Desert, the "desert of deserts," is so hot and dry that even flies can't survive there. For hundreds of miles, everywhere you look, the only things in sight are sand dunes littered with patches of pebbles. But in the middle of this vast Nigerien desert, about 100 miles from anything green, a single spiny acacia tree somehow sprouted up from the sand.

This lonely acacia was so famous that it was included on maps of the region. It was given a name: the Ténéré Tree. Shaped like an umbrella, the tree offered the only bit of shelter on the salt caravan route through the desert. (This is the route that salt traders took from the salt mines in northern Mali to the trading posts of Timbuktu.) The lone tree was so special that nobody was allowed to touch it. A symbol of life for anyone who discovered it, the tree was thought to be about 300 years old.

This special tree grew and thrived thanks to one bit of luck: Its roots had stretched down 100 feet and found an *aquifer* (an underground spring). But the Ténéré Tree also had two bits of bad luck. The first is that in the late 1930s, one of its Y-shaped branches was knocked off during construction of a nearby well.

Then in 1973, a truck managed to crash into the tree, in spite of the fact that it was the only obstacle around for hundreds of miles! The tree could not survive the second accident—its luck had finally run out.

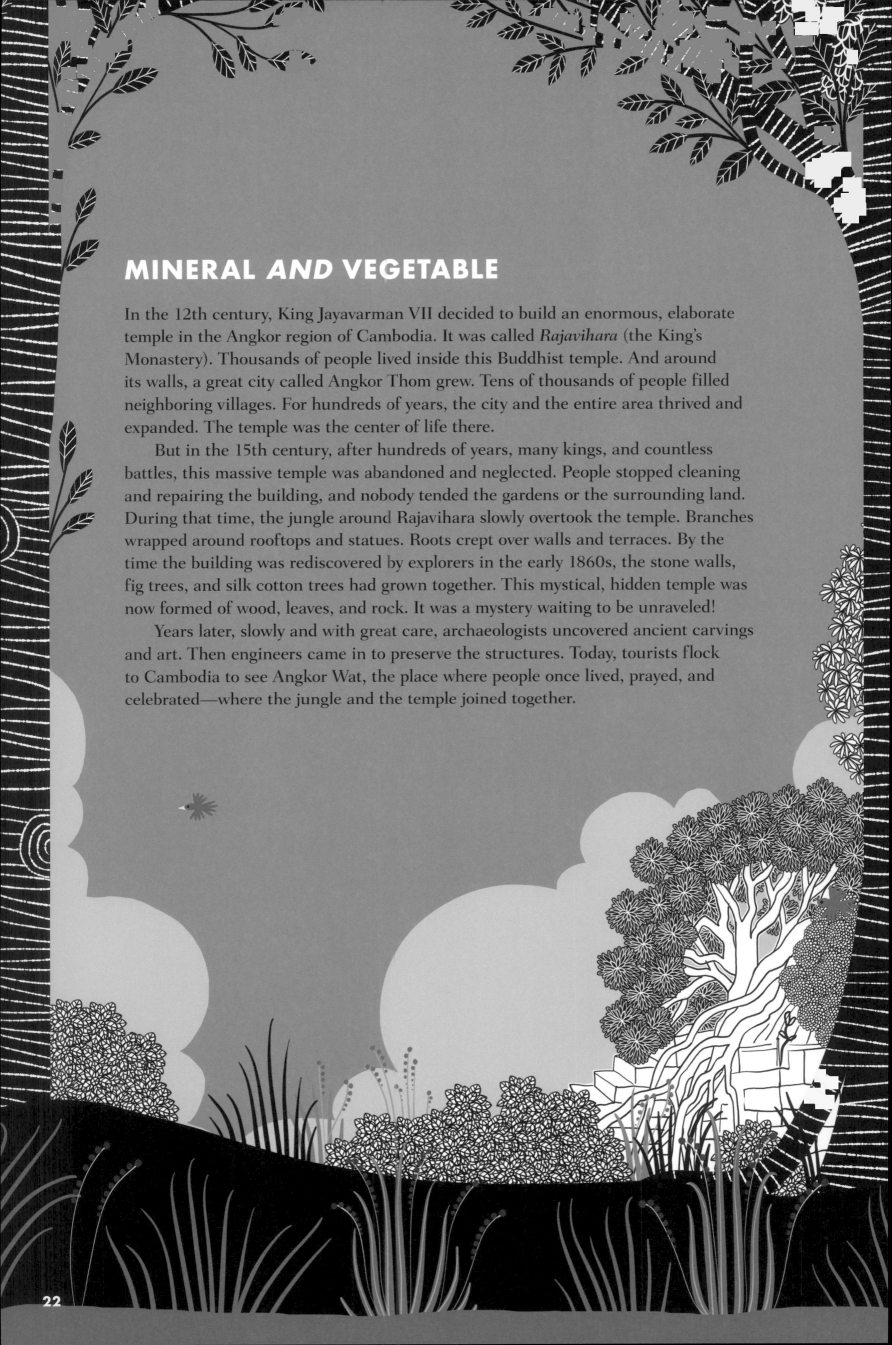

MINERAL *AND* VEGETABLE

In the 12th century, King Jayavarman VII decided to build an enormous, elaborate temple in the Angkor region of Cambodia. It was called *Rajavihara* (the King's Monastery). Thousands of people lived inside this Buddhist temple. And around its walls, a great city called Angkor Thom grew. Tens of thousands of people filled neighboring villages. For hundreds of years, the city and the entire area thrived and expanded. The temple was the center of life there.

But in the 15th century, after hundreds of years, many kings, and countless battles, this massive temple was abandoned and neglected. People stopped cleaning and repairing the building, and nobody tended the gardens or the surrounding land. During that time, the jungle around Rajavihara slowly overtook the temple. Branches wrapped around rooftops and statues. Roots crept over walls and terraces. By the time the building was rediscovered by explorers in the early 1860s, the stone walls, fig trees, and silk cotton trees had grown together. This mystical, hidden temple was now formed of wood, leaves, and rock. It was a mystery waiting to be unraveled!

Years later, slowly and with great care, archaeologists uncovered ancient carvings and art. Then engineers came in to preserve the structures. Today, tourists flock to Cambodia to see Angkor Wat, the place where people once lived, prayed, and celebrated—where the jungle and the temple joined together.

THE ARCHITECTS

THE DOUBLE CHAPEL
In the town of Allouville-Bellefosse, in northern France, there is a very special old oak tree. At more than 800 years old, it is believed to be the oldest tree in France. A tiny chapel was created inside its hollow trunk. Later, a second chapel was built higher up in the trunk, along with a spiral staircase wrapping around the tree. During the French Revolution, a crowd came to burn the tree because it was a symbol of the church. But a village schoolteacher posted a sign on its trunk calling it "The Temple of Reason."

THE PERCH
In Morocco, goats have a favorite snack: the fruit of the argan tree. Once they have finished eating the fallen and low-hanging fruit, these greedy animals will actually climb up the tree to feed! "Goat trees," argan trees filled with goats, can be seen all over southwestern Morocco. Farmers encourage the tree-climbing. After eating, the goats spit out the seeds, and the farmers use the seeds to make argan oil, which is used in skincare products.

THE PRISON
In the town of Wyndham, in southwestern Australia, there stands a giant old boab tree. Its hollow trunk is so spacious that many people could fit inside—and for years rumors spread that it had been used as a prison.

THE COLUMNS
The famous Avenue of the Baobab is found in the western part of Madagascar. Dozens of majestic baobabs, relics of a long-gone forest, line both sides of a yellow dirt road.

THE HIDEOUT
The forest of Brocéliande in Brittany, France, is believed to be King Arthur's enchanted forest. According to legend, one of the oak trees in the forest served as a hiding place for the priest Pierre-Paul Guillotin. It is said that during the French Revolution, he hid in a cavity in the tree's trunk, and every day a spider spun a web over the opening to protect him.

INSIDE THE BAOBAB

In Africa, there are many legends about baobab trees. Their spindly branches, which resemble a root system, have led people to say that the trees were uprooted and planted upside down. Others have said that spirits hide inside the trunks or that baobabs fly and have chosen to land in the villages where they stand.

Most baobabs have a gap in the trunk that a person can step through (should they want to explore inside the tree). Many stories refer to people hiding from enemies in the heart of baobab trees. In Senegal, up until the early 1960s, the Serer people placed the bodies of dead *griots* (storytellers) in the hollow trunks of a cemetery baobab because they believed that burying a griot underground would bring drought.

The baobab is also known as the "pharmacist tree" because its pods, seeds, bark, leaves, sap, and roots are used to cure many ailments, from stomachaches and wounds to coughs and even malaria! Parts of the baobab are also consumed in sauces and as juice and are used in soap and fertilizer. Its fibers are turned into cords and sponges.

A spiritual symbol in Senegal and southern African countries, it's known as the "tree of life." The baobab often serves as a conference tree, where people come together to discuss and resolve conflicts. Because these trees have such a rich history and so many special purposes, nobody would ever cut one down.

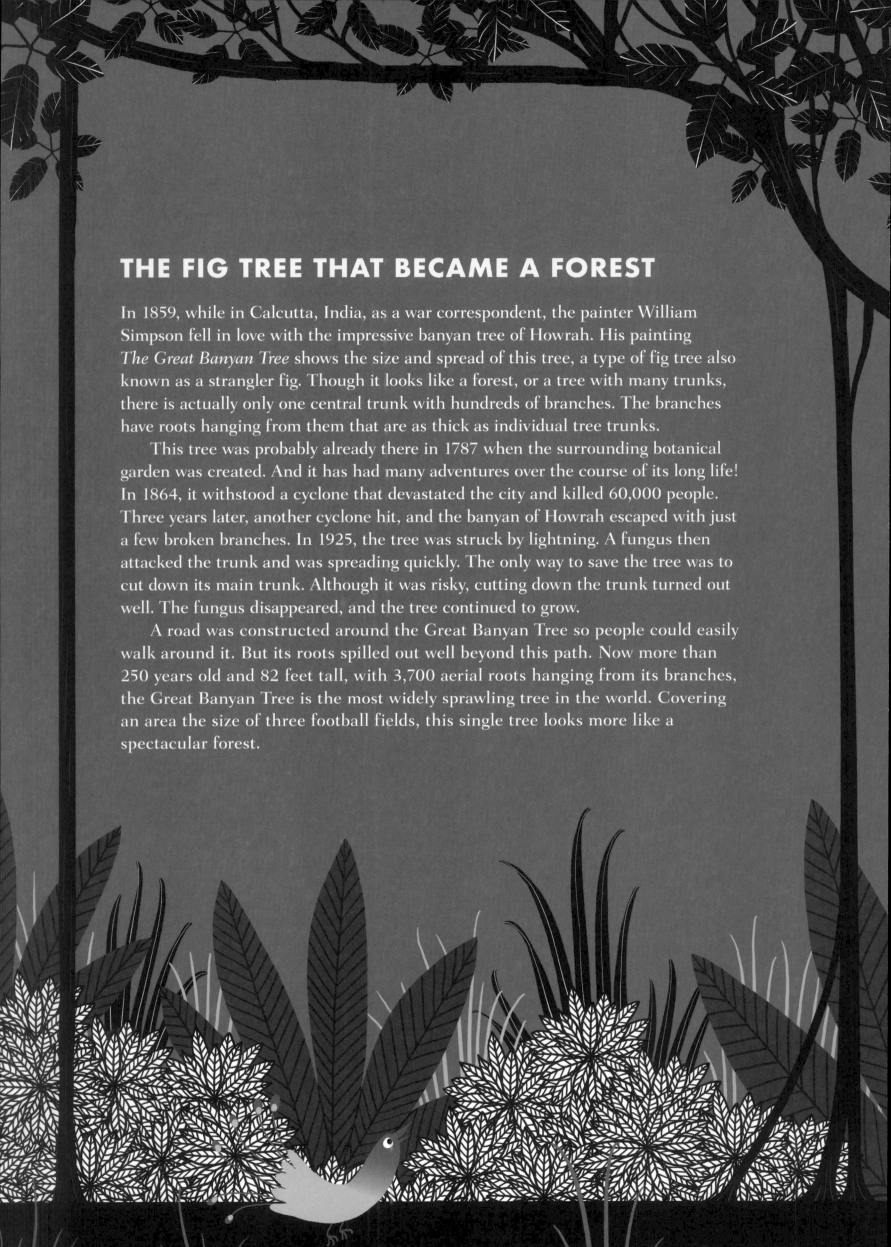

THE FIG TREE THAT BECAME A FOREST

In 1859, while in Calcutta, India, as a war correspondent, the painter William Simpson fell in love with the impressive banyan tree of Howrah. His painting *The Great Banyan Tree* shows the size and spread of this tree, a type of fig tree also known as a strangler fig. Though it looks like a forest, or a tree with many trunks, there is actually only one central trunk with hundreds of branches. The branches have roots hanging from them that are as thick as individual tree trunks.

This tree was probably already there in 1787 when the surrounding botanical garden was created. And it has had many adventures over the course of its long life! In 1864, it withstood a cyclone that devastated the city and killed 60,000 people. Three years later, another cyclone hit, and the banyan of Howrah escaped with just a few broken branches. In 1925, the tree was struck by lightning. A fungus then attacked the trunk and was spreading quickly. The only way to save the tree was to cut down its main trunk. Although it was risky, cutting down the trunk turned out well. The fungus disappeared, and the tree continued to grow.

A road was constructed around the Great Banyan Tree so people could easily walk around it. But its roots spilled out well beyond this path. Now more than 250 years old and 82 feet tall, with 3,700 aerial roots hanging from its branches, the Great Banyan Tree is the most widely sprawling tree in the world. Covering an area the size of three football fields, this single tree looks more like a spectacular forest.

THE GOLDEN SPRUCE AND THE LUMBERJACK

The Haida people, Native Americans of northwestern Canada, believed a certain spruce was actually a young boy turned into a tree for disobeying his grandfather. They called it *K'iid K'iyaas*. Locals called it the "Ooh Aah Tree" for the exclamations of visitors upon first seeing this odd giant with a rare genetic mutation. In the midst of a dense and dark wooded landscape, it sparkled. The spruce had golden needles! Even the local lumberjacks, a tough bunch who did difficult and dangerous work, were extra fond of this tree. Well, *almost* all of the lumberjacks.

On a cold night in January 1997, a man named Thomas Grant Hadwin swam across the freezing Yakoun River with a heavy bag. He clambered up the steep and slippery riverbank and headed for the 165-foot-tall Golden Spruce. This forest engineer then proceeded with his plan: For many hours through the night and into the next day, he used a chainsaw to cut away at the trunk, which measured close to 20 feet around. A few days later, the mighty tree fell over during a windstorm, taking most of the nearby vegetation with it.

The day after it fell, Thomas wrote to newspapers, to Greenpeace, and to the Haida Nation to explain his bizarre actions. He was hoping to express his rage toward people who harm the planet. He was arrested, then released, and ordered to stand trial.

The Haida organized a ceremony to mourn their ancestor. They were joined by neighbors, and together they formed the largest gathering ever in their region. Thomas, on the other hand, never stopped trying to justify his actions, insisting that the majestic Golden Spruce was distracting people from the lumber companies' destruction of the surrounding forest. He did not seem to understand his own act of destruction.

Ultimately, Thomas never showed up at his trial. According to witnesses, he had decided to travel to his trial by kayak to avoid the angry crowds. The remains of his kayak were found, but he was not.

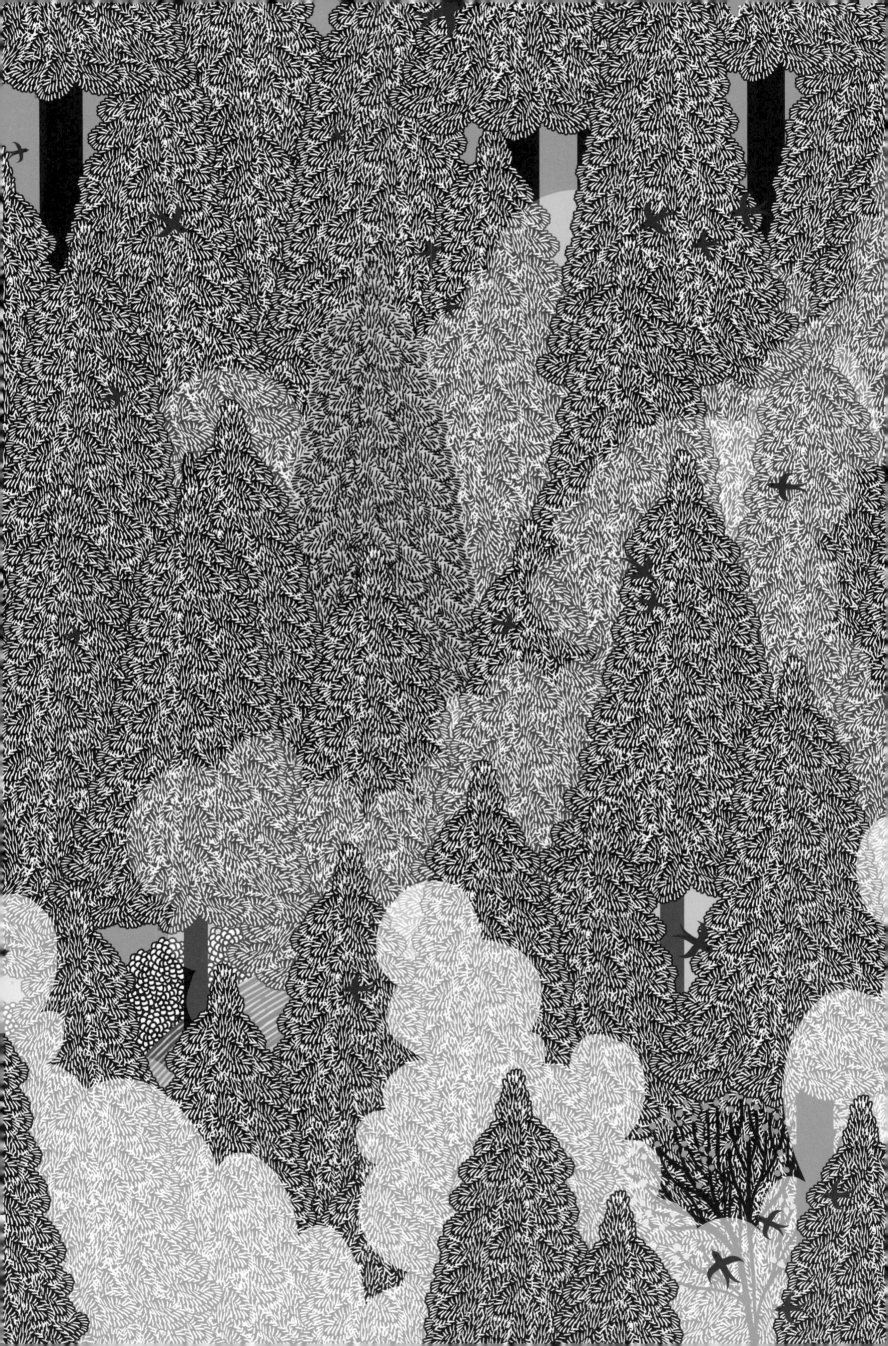

TREE TRADITIONS

WISHES IN THE WIND
In Ireland and northern France, people hang clothes on "rag trees" for luck in curing an illness or solving a problem. The idea is to tie the problem to a branch. A person might choose a handkerchief for a cold or a sock for a broken foot. Similar traditions can be found in Africa and Asia, where people hang wishes written on paper or cloth on trees.

THE COTTON TREE
In 1787, the British founded Freetown in Sierra Leone (a country in West Africa) as a home for freed slaves. The new townspeople gathered to celebrate their freedom with prayer and song at the foot of a kapok, which came to be known as the Cotton Tree. This tree was still there for Sierra Leone's independence day in 1961. It withstood storms as well as gunshots during the country's civil war in the 1990s. Now the Cotton Tree is a symbol of peace and freedom. People leave offerings for ancestors, harmony, and prosperity under this tree.

THE ART OF FLOWER WATCHING
Hanami is the Japanese custom of looking at flowers. In Japan, spring is the season of *hanami,* when the cherry trees blossom in beautiful shades of pink.

FREEDOM
During the French Revolution, "liberty trees" were enthusiastically planted throughout France. One of the most popular liberty trees, the Oak of Saint-Roch, stood in Touraine. In 2009, it had to be cut down because a traffic circle sprawled around it. So two artists, Jean Vindras and Fodé Bayo, created a sculpture that now stands in its place, still symbolizing liberty.

HARMONY
Three trees are twisted together in the center of Mar Lodj, an island in Senegal (a country in West Africa). A silk cotton tree, an African mahogany tree, and a palm tree wrap around one another, forming what is known as "the Sacred Wood." It represents the harmony among the island's three religions: Catholicism, Islam, and Animism. Villagers leave offerings under the trees, and village guides are proud to show them to tourists.

A BONSAI FOR *THE LORD OF THE RINGS*

The art of *bonsai* (the cultivation of miniature trees) was first practiced in China and then in Japan a thousand years ago. People did not make bonsai trees, a natural form of art, in the West until the late 19th century.

The species used to create bonsai trees are found in nature. Bonsai growers use a variety of techniques to control a tree's size, such as pruning roots and training branches.

Chris Guise, a bonsai artist, created a famous bonsai inspired by J.R.R. Tolkien's *The Lord of the Rings*. He started with a live rolled *callus* (a bump) that he cut from a tree. After two years, it was ready for his handiwork! Over the course of some 80 hours, he created a hobbit house and a miniature living landscape— a perfect replica of the movie version, right down to the chimney.

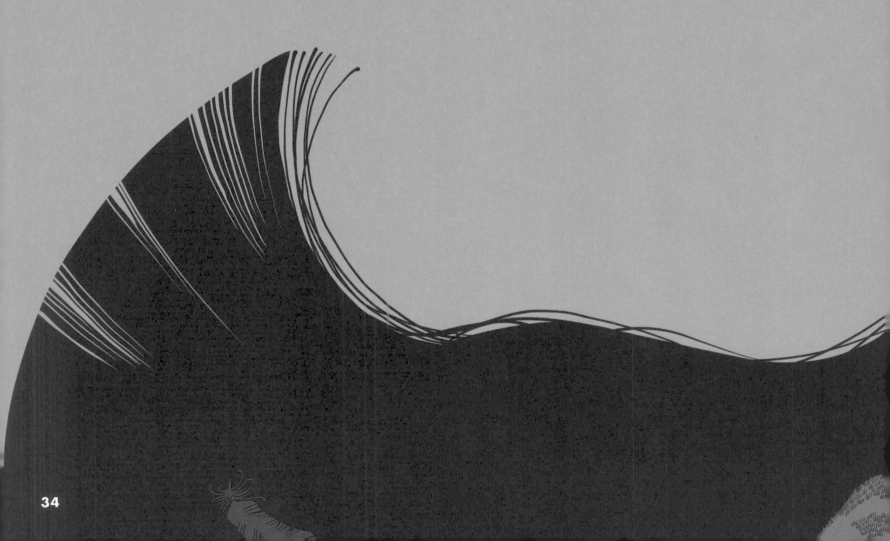

EUCALYPTUS APOCALYPSE

In the humid air that hovers over Tasmania, eucalyptus trees can reach more than 300 feet in height. On this island off the coast of Australia, the forest, known as the Valley of the Giants, had been largely untouched from the time before humans appeared.

But in the 1970s, the noise of machines began to boom in the peaceful, ancient forest. First there was the drone of bulldozers carving a path. Then chainsaws felled the giant eucalyptus trees. Loggers *clear-cut* the forest (removed every tree), destroying huge swaths of green. The enormous tree trunks were cut down, cut up, and pulverized to make paper pulp.

Then came a period of fires, with thick brown smoke engulfing the entire valley for several weeks. Finally, napalm, a poison, was spread over the warm soil. The creatures of the forest—including wallabies, possums, and wombats—disappeared. The majestic valley was replaced by a dry, vast wasteland.

Environmentalists fought hard to protect what was left of the forest. Finally, an agreement was reached in 2013. Now a large part of the Tasmanian forest is protected, designated by UNESCO (the United Nations Educational, Scientific and Cultural Organization) as untouchable.

SAVE LUNA!

This is the story of a young woman who helped save a very old tree. The tree was more than 1,000 years old, and the woman was 23. Its name was Luna, and hers was Julia Butterfly Hill.

Near the town of Stafford, California, the Pacific Lumber Company was planning to cut down some trees. One of those trees, an ancient redwood, stood nearly 200 feet tall. A group of environmental activists called Earth First was determined to stop the loggers from cutting down the tree. They knew that Pacific Lumber couldn't possibly cut down a tree with a person in it! So they built a platform 180 feet up in the branches of the tree, and they looked for a person to sit on it.

Julia loved trees—peaceful hikes through the woods had helped her heal following a serious car accident. She offered to be that person—to live in this tiny treehouse for 30 days. But she was so committed to protecting Luna that she wound up staying for weeks, then months, and eventually, for two years.

Sheltered only by light tarps, she had to deal with rain and freezing cold winters. And the lumber company tried hard to scare her out of the tree. They sent helicopters and men with noisy chainsaws. They shined bright lights into the branches. They even tried to block the people who came to bring her food and supplies. On top of all that, it was lonely up there.

But for Luna, Julia hung on. The tree was her companion, her home, and her friend. There was no question of abandoning it. Finally, Julia's loyalty paid off! After more than two years, the lumber company left. Julia climbed down from her tree after 738 days without setting foot on the ground.

Luna was "the best teacher and friend I've ever had," Julia has said. "The person I'd been when I'd gone up and the person I was when I came down were so profoundly different that I wasn't sure how I was going to be able to live in the world again. . . . Though I left the tree, it's still so much a part of who I am that I can just close my eyes and be in its branches all over again."

THE OLD ONES

THE WRINKLED ONE
At an altitude of nearly 10,000 feet in the White Mountains of California, the exact location of Methuselah is kept secret for its protection. Estimated to be around 4,850 years old, this bristlecone pine is known for its bare and gnarled form. It is, however, alive, and still slowly and peacefully growing.

THE ANCESTOR
Scientists estimate the age of the original root of Old Tjikko at 9,550 years, which makes it one of the oldest freestanding trees in the world. The geologist who discovered this spruce tree on Fulufjället Mountain in Sweden named it after his deceased pet dog.

THE ELDEST
Huon pines grow slowly over a long time and can sometimes reach the impressive age of 2,000. They are among the most ancient tree species on the planet. There is one grove of these Tasmanian pines that is believed to be 10,500 years old!

THE LITTLE OLD GUY
On a hillside in California's Jurupa Mountains grows a bush that measures 75 feet long and 25 feet wide but only about 3 feet tall! Despite its insignificant appearance, this Palmer's oak is more than 13,000 years old.

THE IMMORTAL ONE
Pando is an 80,000-year-old grove of quaking aspens in Utah. Pando has 47,000 trunks, all attached to each other by a massive, interlaced underground root system. It reproduces by cloning, which makes it immortal.

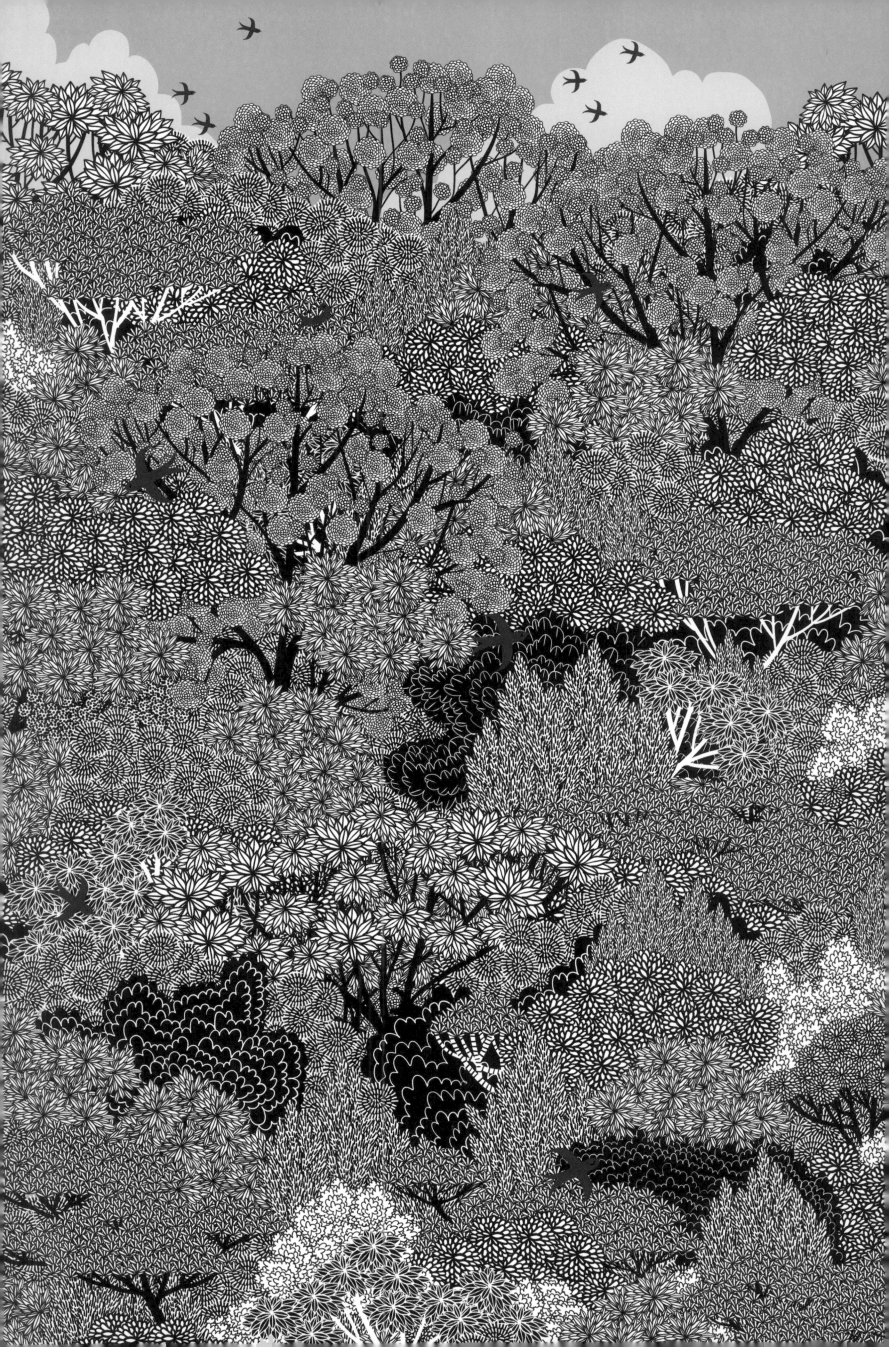